May Your Heart Sing!
Jacquline Shockley
2020

My Heart Sings a Sad Song

Written & Illustrated by

Gary Alan Shockley

Palmetto Publishing Group

Charleston, SC

My Heart Sings a Sad Song

First Edition

Printed in the United States

Hardcover: 978-1-64111-748-7

Softcover: 978-1-64111-834-7

eBook: 978-1-64111-835-4

Acknowledgements

I'm grateful to the many friends who helped with the shaping of this book, especially Amy Styers Bissette, Jason Moore, Joni Robison, and the amazing staff of the Levine Dickson Hospice Houses at Huntersville and Aldersgate in North Carolina. I am grateful to the many patients and families I was privileged to serve who reminded me constantly that life is a precious gift and that thin spaces, where the veil between this world and the next becomes more transparent, are all around us.

Thanks for the love and support of my wife Kim who, in a very short period of time, experienced the death of her parents and grandparents without losing the song of a grateful heart. Together, we sing in remembrance of our loved ones as we learn to live with them in our hearts instead of our arms.

My heart
sings a sad song
because someone
I love has died.

I try to be brave
and sing a glad song

But my heart
just wants to cry.

Everyone says
that I'll be okay

But this minute, I don't
think it's true.

There's an ache
deep inside me, way
down in my heart

And it comes
from being without you.

Where have you gone?
Will I see you again?

Will you miss me?
My heart
needs to know.

Did it hurt
when you left me?

Were you
ready to rest?

Are you where
you wanted to go?

Everyone tells me you're happier now.
But that won't make it easier for me.

My heart
has been broken.
I feel very sad, as sad
as a person can be.

I know that
I love you and
you love me too.
My heart needs
to know this
as well.

So, I'll talk
to my heart
and speak
gentle words.

Many stories about you,
I'll tell.

My family
will help me.
I know that they will.
They'll love me
and care
for my tears.

They'll tell me great stories about how you lived and loved us through all of these years.

Together we'll miss you.
Together we'll heal.
Together we'll love you
and cry.

Together you're with us
deep down in our hearts,
and that is the
best reason why

Someday my heart will sing a new song.
A happy song. It is true.

A song of
remembrance.
A song
full of love.

A song that will celebrate YOU!

Helping Your Child
Grieve the Death of a Loved One

1. Tell the truth about the loved one's death as soon as possible. Children know when something is wrong by the emotions and energy of the adults around them. Use the words dead or died. Phrases such as passed away, lost, gone, or sleeping are confusing and not strong enough to convey reality.

2. Gauge how much your child can process at any given time and share information in small amounts. Accept your child's emotional responses as they are and not what you would wish they'd be, knowing their emotions will vary as they process the death of someone they cared about.

3. Understand that everyone grieves differently. Your child may become silent. They might want to be alone for a while. Some children may act as though nothing has happened. Maybe they will express anger. There is no one right way to grieve.

4. Gently encourage your child to attend the funeral or memorial service and explain what they might expect, especially if there is an open casket. Then gauge whether they are ready for this and do not force them to attend if they are resistant. Encourage your child to help you prepare for the service by gathering photos, collecting tokens of remembrance from trips or visits, selecting songs or a sacred reading. Giving your child a meaningful task might help them gain a sense of control over the loss they are feeling.

5. As much as possible maintain your daily routine and encourage your child to keep up with their usual activities like school, events with friends and other social activities. Keep up family meals and bedtime traditions like story-time, snuggles and prayers.

6. It's good to laugh. Laughter, like crying, is a healing thing. Sharing funny stories and light-hearted remembrances conveys a sense of just how important this person was in your life.

7. Don't put a time limit on your child's (or your own) grieving because grief is a journey and rarely unfolds in a straight path that follows a calendar. Everyone grieves in their own way. A new normal has to develop and time is needed to readjust to a significant death in our lives.

8. Draw from your particular spiritual or religious tradition to explain your thoughts about death. If you feel you need additional support reach out for help. Ask your child's school, your family doctor, or a religious leader you trust to offer assistance.

Space for drawing

Space for writing notes

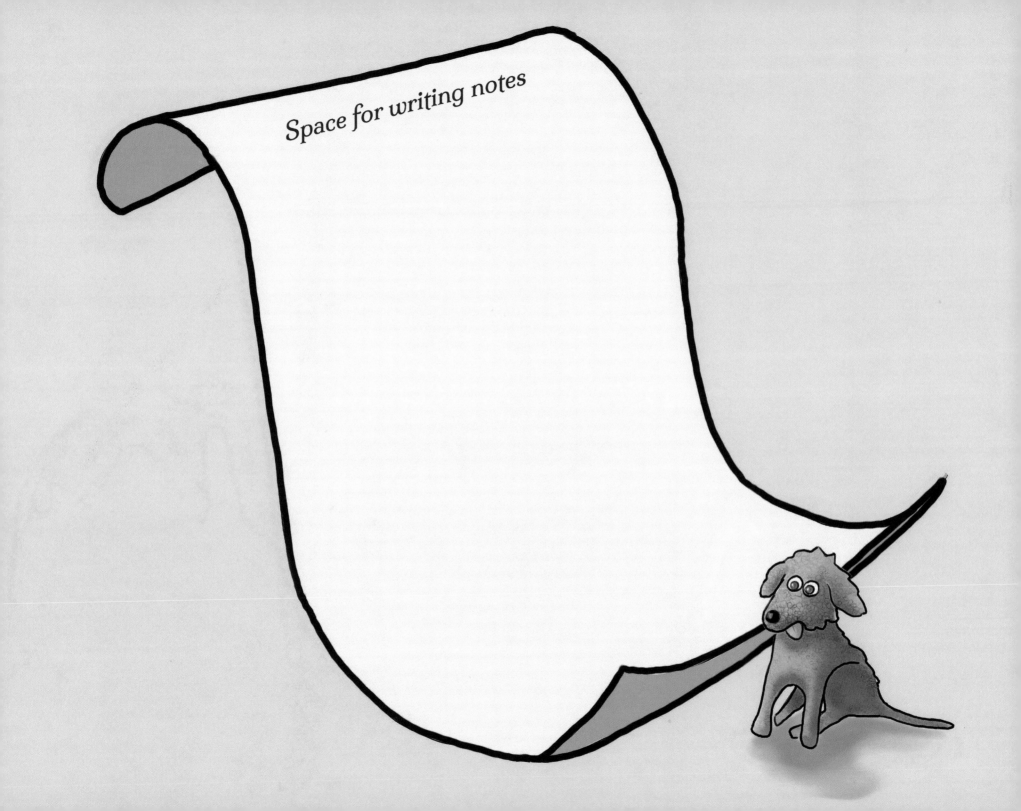

Space for writing notes

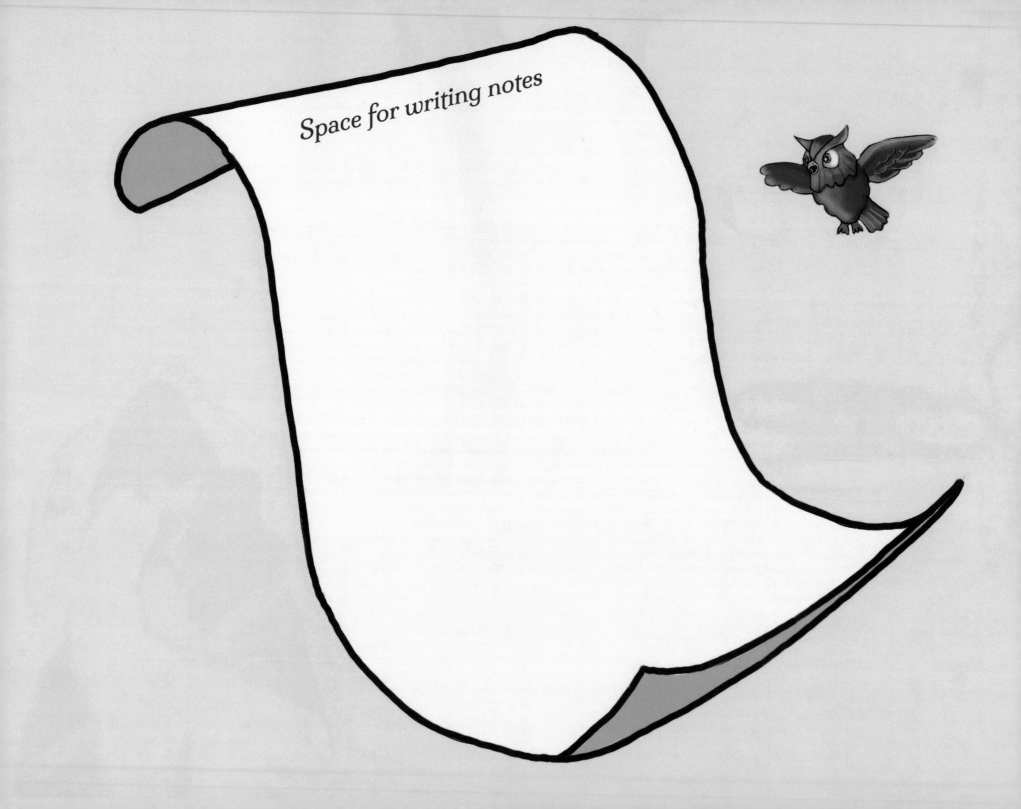

Space for writing notes

CPSIA information can be obtained at www.ICGtesting.com
Printed in the USA
BVIW120731210620
581909BV00002B/3

Using the *Feeling Your Feels* Chart with Children
Gary Alan Shockley ©HopeSpring.biz

Knowing ourselves emotionally can help us recognize the feelings in others which fosters empathy.

Until about age 11, children often struggle with understanding and explaining their feelings, and as a result may act out inappropriately. Without the cognitive reasoning skills required to recognize and verbally discuss what they feel, children are confused about what behavior is appropriate for which emotion. For example, a child may act like they are angry when what they are really feeling is afraid. If they can identify being afraid then an adult can talk to them about their fear rather than address what may seem to be anger.

A very simple and practical way to assist your child in communicating what they are feeling is with this *Feeling Your Feels* Chart. The chart shows nine different primary feelings that your child may experience throughout the day. You may invite them, when you sense it is appropriate, to look at the chart and point to one of JoJo Bunny's faces that illustrate how they are feeling in that moment. Listen for what that feeling means to them and ask them questions about that feeling. Reassure them that feelings are neither right nor wrong. What matters is what we do with our feelings in a healthy way.

A helpful thing for adults is to practice reflecting a child's feelings back to them and validating their emotions. An example is "You were really angry about that" or "That made you very excited!". Try to match your tone to their feeling. Another way to process their feelings can also be "I wonder what would have made that less scary" (or hurtful, etc.) or "I wonder what feelings go with the one you felt" (happy with excited, angry with sad, etc.).

Using the *Feeling Your Feels* chart at night before bed may help a child identify the variety of feelings they experienced during the day. You can talk about how normal this is for all of us and even celebrate the gift of our ability to feel our feels!

Visit www.hopespring.biz for blogs and other helpful guidance!

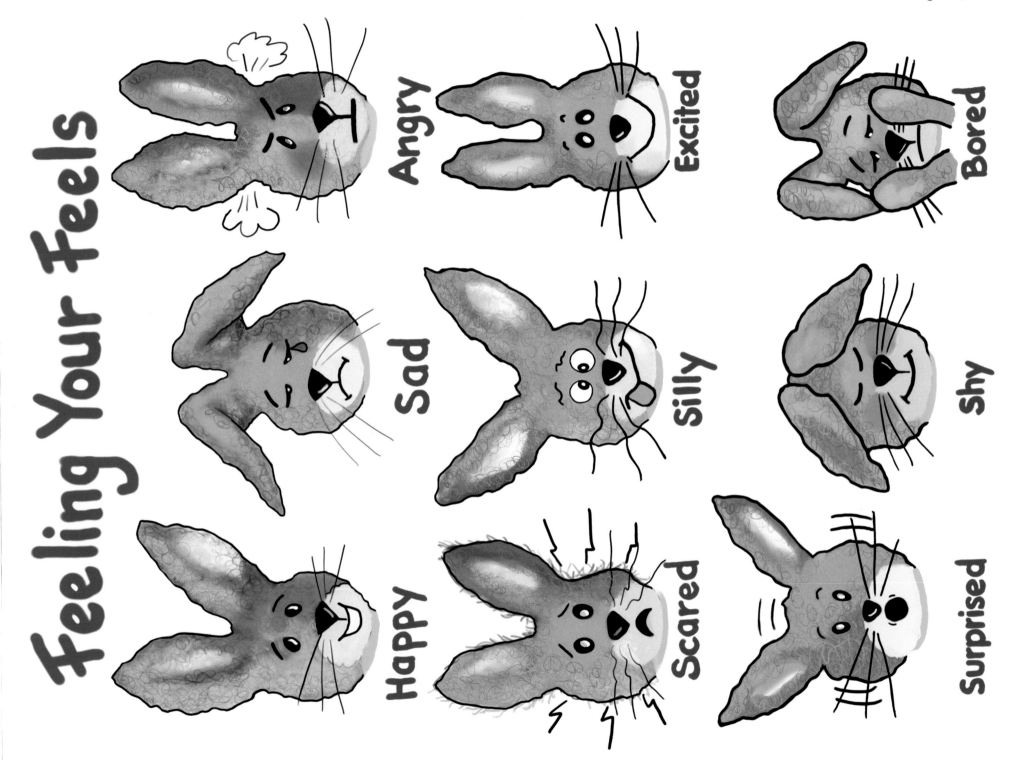

Feeling Your Feels

Angry

Excited

Bored

Sad

Silly

Shy

Happy

Scared

Surprised